PRAYING FROM GOD'S HEART

Experiencing The Power Of God-Focused Prayer

LEE BRASE WITH HENRY HELSABECK

NAVPRESS

BRINGING TRUTH TO LIFE

NavPress Publishing Group

P.O. Box 35001, Colorado Springs, Colorado 80935

The Navigators is an international Christian organization. Jesus Christ gave His followers the Great Commission to go and make disciples (Matthew 28:19). The aim of The Navigators is to help fulfill that commission by multiplying laborers for Christ in every nation.

NavPress is the publishing ministry of The Navigators. NavPress publications are tools to help Christians grow. Although publications alone cannot make disciples or change lives, they can help believers learn biblical discipleship, and apply what they learn to their lives and ministries.

Cover Design: Larry Smith and Associates

Printed in the United States of America

FOR A FREE CATALOG OF
NAVPRESS BOOKS & BIBLE STUDIES,
CALL 1-800-366-7788 (USA)
or 1-416-499-4615 (CANADA)

CONTENTS

How to Use This Guide

Do you ever wonder if you are praying scripturally?

Do you feel an increasing hunger to go deeper in prayer?

Do you need some help in responding to such a hunger to pray?

Would you like to grow in prayer with a group of friends?

Are you interested in what God's thoughts and feelings have to do with prayer?

If you respond positively to these questions, then *Praying From God's Heart* is meant for you. Its aim is to make you an "author" of God-focused prayer, not an "authority" on God-focused prayer. In other words, the goal is to prepare you to *do* prayer rather than to teach prayer.

THE WORKBOOK'S DESIGN

Praying From God's Heart emphasizes experiential learning within a group setting. The workbook is designed for groups of two to twelve people; larger groups may want to divide into subgroups for discussion and prayer.

Each study (except study 1 and study 9) contains the following elements:

▶ *sharing experiences* relating to the previous session,
▶ discussing a *prayer focus,*
▶ discussing the analysis of *a prayer from Scripture,*

5

▶ analyzing *other prayers* from Scripture,
▶ discussing a sample *contemporary prayer*,
▶ discussing the *application* of the prayer focus to your own situations,
▶ *praying* together.

The assignment sections of each study will help you to apply the focus of that study in your personal prayer.

The workbook is structured into two tracks: sixteen sessions and nine sessions. Groups that choose the sixteen-session track will work through every section of the workbook. Groups that choose the nine-session track will omit all sections in shaded boxes. If your group adheres to the minimum times allotted for each section, then each session (except for the first and last) in the sixteen-week track will take sixty minutes and each session in the nine-week track will take ninety minutes. You will find suggested time schedules for each session in each track on pages 7-8.

Most groups will find the sixteen-session track to provide the most comfortable pace. However, if your group consists of only two people, you may find the nine-session track to provide the optimal pace.

FACILITATOR LEADERSHIP
This workbook is designed to be used without trained leadership. However, it is important to have a facilitator to keep the sessions moving at an acceptable pace. The facilitator should do three things to prepare for each session:

1. PRAY for each member of the group before your group meets, asking God to open his or her spiritual eyes to see God's perspective more clearly as you meet together. (Praying a specific scripture for them is an especially effective way to lift this request up to God.)

2. READ through the material for the session you are facilitating. For material that is to be read, decide how your group will do this: have a single member read a given section aloud; have several members take turns reading aloud; or have the group read the section silently. In some sections, instructions are given as to which to do, but your group may be more comfortable with its own preference.

3. PLAN a tentative time schedule for the session(s). You may photocopy the schedules listed below and fill in appropriate times for each section. (Use the column corresponding to the track your group is using.) The numbers in parentheses give suggested minimum times for each section. If you can list actual clock times for each section (such as 8:20–8:40), you will find it easier to keep to your schedule.

Our prayer for you as you undertake this experience in God-focused prayer is the same as Paul's prayer to the Christians at Ephesus, "that the God of our Lord Jesus Christ, the glorious Father, may give you the Spirit of wisdom and revelation, so that you may know him better . . . that the eyes of your heart may be enlightened in order that you may know . . . his incomparably great power for us who believe. That power is like the working of his mighty strength" (Ephesians 1:17-19).

TIME SCHEDULES
Study 1
Both Tracks
Opening (10 minutes)

Prayer Focus (40 minutes)

Group Prayer (25 minutes)

   Total (75 minutes)

Studies 2 through 8

16-Session Track
(Two Sessions per Study)   **9-Session Track**

❖ PART A ❖
First Session

Sharing (15 minutes)   Sharing (15 minutes)

Group Prayer (10 minutes)

The Prayer Focus (20 minutes)	The Prayer Focus (15 minutes)
The Prayer (15 minutes)	The Prayer (15 minutes)
Total (60 minutes)	

❖ PART B ❖

Second Session

Review (15 minutes)

Another Prayer (10 minutes)	Another Prayer (15 minutes)
A Prayer for Our Time (5 minutes)	A Prayer for Our Time (5 minutes)
Group Prayer (30 minutes)	Group Prayer (25 minutes)
Total (60 minutes)	Total (90 minutes)

Study 9
Both Tracks

Sharing (20 minutes)

Convictions (15 minutes)

Group Prayer (30 minutes)

Future Plans (10 minutes)

Total (75 minutes)

INTRODUCTION TO GOD-FOCUSED INTERCESSION
Psalm 25

OPENING (10 minutes)
Choose someone to facilitate this group discussion.

1. If your group members are not well acquainted with one another, introduce yourselves.

2. Have each participant tell what he or she hopes to get from this study.

3. Give each person a chance to share a significant experience he or she has had with prayer.

THE PRAYER FOCUS (40 minutes)
Have a volunteer read the following section of text aloud. Then discuss question 4 aloud. You may take turns reading subsequent sections aloud or read them silently.

God's Call to Prayer
The great Bible teacher Matthew Henry once said, "When God intends great mercies for His people, He first of all sets them a'praying."

How many times have you heard someone say something similar to these statements: "God has been giving me a heart to pray more" or "God has been leading me to pray more deeply"? Perhaps you have made such comments. This study guide is for people whose hearts have been touched with the God-given desire to go deeper with Him in intercession—to experience a God-centered intercession that can advance His Kingdom in the world as well as within the heart of the intercessor.

Most of the great works of God have occurred after people have prayed. Consider, for example, the forgiveness of Israel after making the golden calf (Exodus 32) and the outpouring of God's Spirit at Pentecost (Acts 1–2).

4. Recall other works of God that you can directly relate to people praying:

▶ In the Bible

▶ In history

▶ In your personal experience

God-Focused Intercession
In the publisher's foreword of *If You Will Ask*, Oswald Chamber's thoughts were summarized: "Prayer is getting ourselves attuned to God, not getting God attuned to us. It is developing the life of God in us."[1] In the same book, Chambers wrote, "The purpose of prayer is to reveal the presence of God."[2]

In the 150 psalms, the nouns *Lord* and *God* are mentioned more than 1,200 times. No other subject comes close. Although the psalmists often wrote during times of agony, they still brought God into focus.

In teaching the disciples to pray, Jesus prayed a God-focused prayer. At least half of the prayer relates to God's per-

son and desires. Man's needs are not the central concern.
Jesus offered two invitations:

▶ "Come to me, all you who are weary and burdened"
  (Matthew 11:28).
▶ "My soul is overwhelmed with sorrow to the point of
  death. Stay here and keep watch with me" (Matthew
  26:38).

The first invitation focuses on us and our needs. The second
focuses on our Lord and His desires. Both invitations are
open to us. The content of this workbook relates to the
Lord's second invitation: to have Him as our primary focus in
intercession.

Numbers 13–14 illustrates the powerful effect of having
God as our primary focus. Before Israel went into Canaan,
Moses sent twelve spies to explore the land. When they
returned, ten focused on how big the people and walls were.
Because of this, their faith was small. The other two focused
on how big God was. This focus caused them to believe that
the problem of giants and walls could be overcome.

We hope this workbook will help you develop a style of
intercession that is focused primarily on God.

5. How is God-focused praying different from need-focused
   praying?

Co-Laboring with God

Intercession reflects a principle of God that He set forth from
the beginning: the principle of co-laborship. God decided that
He would make humans in His own image and give them the
responsibility to co-labor with Him here on earth. Obviously
He didn't need the help of humans, but He chose to use them
in this way. From the work given Adam in the Garden of Eden

to this day, God has called people to cooperate with Him in His work.

In 1 Corinthians 3:5-9, Paul describes the division of spiritual labor as he compared the work of God with the work of farming. Paul planted the seed, Apollos watered it, and God made it grow. God could have done it all, but He chose to allow humans to have a significant role (in fact, a necessary role) in the process.

This principle of co-laborship is strongly present in God's design for intercession. A vivid example of the co-laborship between God and man through intercession is the battle between the armies of Israel and the Amalekites (Exodus 17). The outcome of the battle was determined not by how well the armies were fighting, but by whether or not Moses' hands were "lifted up to the throne of the LORD." God determined the outcome based upon the intercession of Moses—upon the partnership of Moses' intercession.

As we will discover in this study, intercession involves a thoughtful process in pleading a case before God and a scriptural understanding of the mind of God. This work will involve praise and thanksgiving, confession and repentance, standing firm and waging war.

6. What are some other examples—in the Bible or your own experience—where you see God and human beings laboring together?

Learning to Pray: Pray!
The philosophy of this study is well articulated by Samuel Chadwick in *The Path of Prayer*:

> There is no way to learn to pray but by praying. No reasoned philosophy of prayer ever taught a soul to pray. The subject is beset with problems, but there are no problems of prayer to the man who prays . . . and if prayer waits for understanding it will never begin.[3]

Isn't this philosophy verified by the Lord Jesus Himself in His response to His disciples' request, "Lord, teach us to pray"? His response was not a teaching on prayer—it was a prayer. The way to learn to pray is *to pray*.

Another philosophy of this study is that the best examples of intercession are to be found in God's Word. Each session will focus on one or more of the prayers in Scripture. We will let the biblical intercessors be our mentors as we develop our experience with God in intercession.

7. If you could pray with someone from the Bible (besides Jesus) or someone you know, who would it be? Why would you choose that person?

GROUP PRAYER (25 minutes)
8. Read Psalm 25:1-15 together.

> [1]To you, O LORD, I lift up my soul;
>> [2]in you I trust, O my God.
> Do not let me be put to shame,
>> nor let my enemies triumph over me.
> [3]No one whose hope is in you
>> will ever be put to shame,
> but they will be put to shame
>> who are treacherous without excuse.
> [4]Show me your ways, O LORD,
>> teach me your paths;
> [5]guide me in your truth and teach me,
>> for you are God my Savior,
>> and my hope is in you all day long.
> [6]Remember, O LORD, your great mercy and love,
>> for they are from of old.
> [7]Remember not the sins of my youth
>> and my rebellious ways;
> according to your love remember me,
>> for you are good, O LORD.
> [8]Good and upright is the LORD;
>> therefore he instructs sinners in his ways.

⁹He guides the humble in what is right
and teaches them his way.
¹⁰All the ways of the LORD are loving and faithful
for those who keep the demands of his covenant.
¹¹For the sake of your name, O LORD,
forgive my iniquity, though it is great.
¹²Who, then, is the man that fears the LORD?
He will instruct him in the way chosen for him.
¹³He will spend his days in prosperity,
and his descendants will inherit the land.
¹⁴The LORD confides in those who fear him;
he makes his covenant known to them.
¹⁵My eyes are ever on the LORD,
for only he will release my feet from the snare.

9. What did the psalmist believe about God?

10. What, specifically, did the psalmist ask God to do?

11. Pray together as a group, using thoughts from Psalm 25.

TRACK DECISION
Decide which of the two tracks your group will follow. Groups of more than two members will likely find the pace of the six-teen-session track to be the more comfortable of the two.

Decide how your group will handle the facilitation of each session. Will there be one facilitator, or will you take turns?

ASSIGNMENT
12. Spend time each day praying about this study. Ask God to teach you what He wants you to learn, and tell Him you are willing to do what He asks you to do. Record any thoughts you would like to share with the group.

13. Read through the Prayer Focus section in study 2.

14. Write an answer to this question before the next session: What have you seen God do this week?

Notes
1. Publisher's Foreword to *If You Will Ask* by Oswald Chambers (Grand Rapids, MI: Discovery House Publishers/Chosen Books, 1985), page 1.
2. Chambers, page 10.
3. Samuel Chadwick, *The Path of Prayer* (London: Hodder and Stoughton, 1931), page 18.

FOCUSING ON GOD THROUGH PRAISE
Psalm 63

❖ PART A ❖

SHARING (15 minutes)

1. Share what you have seen God do this past week. Relate one or more items you recorded in exercise 14 of last session's assignment.

2. How do people praise God? Give some examples.

3. How do *you* praise God?

Groups following the nine-session track should omit shaded sections of each study.

THE PRAYER FOCUS: *Focusing on God Through Praise*
(15 minutes [9 sessions] or 20 minutes [16 sessions])

Have you ever thought about the volume of praise offered at the birth of Jesus? *Mary* composed a song of praise (Luke 1:46-55). *John the Baptist* leaped in his mother's womb (1:41). "A great company of the *heavenly host*" praised God as they announced Christ's birth (2:13-14). The *shepherds* went to see the Christ child and then "returned, glorifying and praising God" (2:15-20). At the temple, *Simeon* "took him in his arms and praised God" (2:28-32). The prophetess *Anna* "gave thanks to God" (2:36-38). When the *Magi* saw Jesus "they bowed down and worshiped him" (Matthew 2:11).

It would seem more logical that such praise would *follow* the life and victories of Christ rather than precede them. If the only purpose of praise were to celebrate, then such praise would certainly come after victory and not before. But there is an aspect of praise that many of us have missed, a truth about praise that the saints of old understood. If we grasp this truth, it will greatly enhance the effectiveness of our intercession. That truth is that *praise opens the door for God's rule.*

The King of kings is "enthroned on the praises" of His people (Psalm 22:3). When we offer praise, we open the door for God to rule. This is precisely what happened at the birth of Jesus. All that praise brought the throne of God, or the rule of God, to bear on all that surrounded our Lord's birth.

Not only was Jesus birthed amid praise, so was the church. From the ascension of Christ until Pentecost, the apostles "stayed continually at the temple, praising God" (Luke 24:53). According to Acts 13:1-3, the work of missions was also birthed "while they were worshiping the Lord and fasting."

The enemy cannot reign where God is enthroned. There can be only one ruler. Praise proclaims God's rule and displaces Satan's.

A clear example of praise opening the door for God's rule happened in Judah while Jehoshaphat was king. Three armies surrounded Judah. Jehoshaphat proclaimed a fast and a prayer meeting. After prayer, God's people were assured of victory. Then we are told, "Jehoshaphat appointed men to sing to the LORD and to praise him for the splendor of his holiness as they went out at the head of the army" (2 Chronicles 20:21). The very next verse says, "As they began to sing and praise, the

LORD set ambushes against" the enemy.

Perhaps the most helpless being on earth is an infant. Yet with praise a little child can defeat the most powerful enemy of darkness.

> From the lips of children and infants
>> you have ordained praise
> because of your enemies,
>> to silence the foe and the avenger. (Psalm 8:2)

The next time you hear a child singing or praising God, consider what impact this may be having in the heavenly realm at that moment.

4. Share one thought that stood out to you from this reading.

THE PRAYER: *Psalm 63* (15 minutes)

A volunteer should read this psalm aloud, then group members can read the analysis silently.

> [1]O God, you are my God,
>> earnestly I seek you;
> my soul thirsts for you,
>> my body longs for you,
> in a dry and weary land
>> where there is no water.
> [2] I have seen you in the sanctuary
>> and beheld your power and your glory.
> [3]Because your love is better than life,
>> my lips will glorify you.
> [4]I will praise you as long as I live,
>> and in your name I will lift up my hands.
> [5]My soul will be satisfied as with the richest of foods;
>> with singing lips my mouth will praise you.

^{6}On my bed I remember you;
    I think of you through the watches of the night.
^{7}Because you are my help,
    I sing in the shadow of your wings.
^{8}My soul clings to you;
    your right hand upholds me.
^{9}They who seek my life will be destroyed;
    they will go down to the depths of the earth.
^{10}They will be given over to the sword
    and become food for jackals.
^{11}But the king will rejoice in God;
    all who swear by God's name will praise him,
    while the mouths of liars will be silenced.

Praise is the focus of many of the psalms, and Psalm 63 is one of these praise psalms. But the context of this psalm makes its praise an "enthroning" praise. David offered this psalm to God when David's life was threatened in the desert of Judah. It was not the praise of celebration because not much was happening in David's physical life that would cause one to celebrate.

But we can see that praise dominates the text. The majority of the verses have praise for God; most of the rest of the verses declare the psalmist's desire for God. Only in the last three verses is there any mention of the dire straits in which the psalmist finds himself. Even there, we see a final exultation of victory as David declares that "all who swear by God's name will praise him."

Consider these wonderful phrases of praise and adoration that David offers to God from the harshness of the desert:

▶ "You are my God"
▶ "Earnestly I seek you"
▶ "My soul thirsts for you"
▶ "My body longs for you"
▶ "I have . . . beheld your power and your glory"
▶ "Your love is better than life"
▶ "My lips will glorify you"
▶ "I will praise you as long as I live"
▶ "In your name I will lift up my hands"

- ▶ "My soul will be satisfied as with the richest of foods"
- ▶ "With singing lips my mouth will praise you"
- ▶ "On my bed I remember you"
- ▶ "I think of you through the watches of the night"
- ▶ "I sing in the shadow of your wings"
- ▶ "My soul clings to you"
- ▶ "Your right hand upholds me"

Each of these pronouncements is like a blow of a mighty sword against the enemy. Satan cannot stand against such an assault. At the same time, these pronouncements are like the palms laid down before Jesus to usher Him as Messiah into the City of the Great King.

Isn't it time that we, as intercessors, use the mighty tool of praise to dethrone the enemy and enthrone our God?

5. Briefly share your own thoughts on this psalm.

ASSIGNMENT (homework for the 16-week track only)
▶ Work through the "Another Prayer" section in Part B of this study by reading the Scripture and answering the questions.
▶ Answer this question before the next session: What have you seen God do this week? Write your answer below.

Focusing on God Through Praise

❖ PART B ❖

REVIEW (15 minutes)
▶ Share what you have seen God do this past week. Relate one or more items you recorded in exercise 2 of last session's assignment.
▶ Review together what you learned in your last session from this study's "Prayer Focus" section.

ANOTHER PRAYER (15 minutes [9 sessions] or 10 minutes [16 sessions])

Read Psalm 108:

¹My heart is steadfast, O God;
    I will sing and make music with all my soul.
²Awake, harp and lyre!
    I will awaken the dawn.
³I will praise you, O LORD, among the nations;
    I will sing of you among the peoples.
⁴For great is your love, higher than the heavens;
    your faithfulness reaches to the skies.
⁵Be exalted, O God, above the heavens,
    and let your glory be over all the earth.
⁶Save us and help us with your right hand,
    that those you love may be delivered.
⁷God has spoken from his sanctuary:
    "In triumph I will parcel out Shechem
    and measure off the Valley of Succoth.
⁸Gilead is mine, Manasseh is mine;
    Ephraim is my helmet,
    Judah my scepter.
⁹Moab is my washbasin,
    upon Edom I toss my sandal;
    over Philistia I shout in triumph."
¹⁰Who will bring me to the fortified city?
    Who will lead me to Edom?
¹¹Is it not you, O God, you who have rejected us
    and no longer go out with our armies?

[12]Give us aid against the enemy,
  for the help of man is worthless.
[13]With God we will gain the victory,
  and he will trample down our enemies.

6. Analyze this prayer together.

 a. What did David believe about God?

 b. How did David honor or exalt God?

 c. What results did David expect?

In your future Bible reading, be alert to Scriptures that use praise to enthrone God.

A PRAYER FOR OUR TIME (5 minutes)

Have a volunteer read the following aloud:

   Suppose that through a reorganization of the company for which you work, you find yourself under a new management team. Suppose also that for various reasons (some of them caused by you, but most caused by others who have been looking for a chance to attack you), you are in deep trouble with this team of supervisors. In fact, there is a good chance that you will lose not only your job, but also your opportunities to get another one in the same industry.

You may not feel like praising God, but could this be an opportunity to enthrone God through praise? Consider praying like this (see Psalm 27):

O God, You are my light and my salvation; whom shall I fear? You are the stronghold of my life; of whom shall I be afraid? When my adversaries attack me, saying slanderous things against me, they will stumble and fall. Though the whole company, even the whole industry, come against me, my heart will not fear, for I will be confident.

Lord, I only ask one thing of You; that's all I really want. May I dwell in Your presence all the days of my life, so that I may behold Your beauty? For in Your presence I find joy; in Your presence I find shelter; in Your presence I am lifted high upon the Rock, the Rock of my Savior, Jesus Christ.

And now my head will be lifted up above my enemies all around me, and I will offer to God sacrifices with shouts of joy. I will sing and make melody to the Lord. I praise You, my Rock and my Salvation!

GROUP PRAYER (25 minutes [9 sessions] or 30 minutes [16 sessions])

7. Briefly share one or more issues for which you would like the group to intercede.

8. Enter a time of praise using Psalm 108 as a basis. Do not address the concerns just shared, but rather believe that your praises are "enthroning" the rule of God over these concerns. If it is helpful, use one or more of the following steps to allow the psalmists to mentor you.

   a. Repeat their exact words as expressions of your thoughts to God.

   b. Enlarge on what the psalmists say. For example, if they say God is great, you can expand on that by saying such things as, "You made the universe. You control everything. You are greater than all the armies. . . ."

24

c. Sing some of the psalms to the Lord.

d. Make a list of God's titles and characteristics mentioned in the psalms. Use these to build your own set of thoughts and writings to God.

Please remember that we are dealing with only one function of praise. The Bible presents other powerful functions of praise besides enthroning God.

FINAL THOUGHT
Praise is a part of intercession. Do you know a Christian who is in the midst of a struggle? Instead of giving God requests, try giving Him praise.

ASSIGNMENT
9. Read and think about the following passages of Scripture. Note how praise was used to enthrone God during times of struggle.

Psalm 13

Psalm 22:1-8,22-31

Habakkuk 3:16-19

10. Each day of the week that you spend time in intercession, start with a psalm of praise. Use some of the psalms mentioned in this study, but feel free here to include a psalm whose context is not necessarily a prelude to God's deliverance.

As you intercede this week, begin with one of these psalms. If it is helpful, use the steps given in "Group Prayer" above to allow the psalmists to mentor you.

11. Read the "Prayer Focus" section of study 3.

12. Answer this question before the next session: What have you seen God do this week?

FOCUSING ON GOD'S CHARACTER
2 Chronicles 20

❖ PART A ❖

SHARING (15 minutes)

1. What have you seen God do during this past week? Relate one or more items you recorded in exercise 4 of last session's assignment.

2. What happened this past week during your times of prayer when you tried to focus on God through praise? Recount some of your experiences.

3. Write down one thing you learned from this discussion.

Remember that only groups in the sixteen-session track should do the shaded sections of this study.

GROUP PRAYER (10 minutes)
Pray together, focusing on God through praise.

THE PRAYER FOCUS: *Focusing on God's Character*

(15 minutes [9 sessions] or 20 minutes [16 sessions])

The depth of our intercession is related to the depth of our understanding of God and His character. As we meditate on God's titles and attributes, we can grasp what He desires to do. Then our prayers are based primarily on who God is, not on what we see as human needs.

Let's look at how God's character influenced Jesus' prayer in Luke 11. When the disciples asked Jesus to teach them to pray, He simply prayed. His prayer did not start with the needs of people. He started with a focus on God as Father.

The title *Father* tells us much about God's character. It reveals that He cares about us and takes responsibility for us. As our Father, He desires what is best for us and loves us so much that He disciplines us for our own good. He is approachable and is involved in all aspects of our lives.

No doubt Jesus meditated much on the concept that God is our Father. In Luke 11:2-4, He builds an entire prayer around the fatherhood of God. This prayer is not built so much on the question, "What do people need?" as on the question, "What does our loving heavenly Father want to do?"

The three requests in this prayer are best understood when we realize what a loving father would want for his children:

- ▶ That his children have proper provision—Jesus prays, "Give us each day our daily bread."
- ▶ That his children live together in harmony—Jesus prays, "Forgive us our sins, for we also forgive everyone who sins against us."
- ▶ That his children be protected from harm and danger—Jesus prays, "And lead us not into temptation, but deliver us from the evil one."

The great intercessors in history knew God well. The chief infuence on their prayers was what they saw and knew of God. Isaiah saw our Lord's holiness and cried out, "Woe to me! . . . I am ruined! For I am a man of unclean lips, and I live among a people of unclean lips, and my eyes have seen the King, the LORD Almighty" (Isaiah 6:5). At that point, Isaiah was prepared in God's eyes to respond to His call.

Jesus addresses God as Father, then develops His prayer consistently around that title. Nehemiah addresses God as "the great and awesome God, who keeps his covenant of love with those who love him and obey his commands" (Nehemiah 1:5). His prayer is built around this concept of God.

The God we Christians worship has one name: Yahweh. That name derives from *who He is* (I Am, the One who is actively present always and everywhere). God also has many titles, all of them derived from *what He does*: Creator, Provider, Holy One, Lord of Hosts. Further, the Scriptures note many of God's attributes: just, merciful, loving, righteous, powerful, and wise.

One of the best ways to honor God is to get a good look at Him and then by faith to pray His desires to take place on earth. Instead of using God to get our desires, we pray for His desires to be accomplished on earth. To intercede in this way, we need to do three things:

▶ Prayerfully meditate on what God is like. We can do this by meditating on one of His titles or attributes.
▶ In light of what you discover about God, ask Him: "What would You like to do?" Allow God to plant thoughts into your heart and mind.
▶ Take the thoughts from God and turn them into prayer.

4. Share one thought that stood out to you from this reading.

THE PRAYER: *2 Chronicles 20:5-12* (15 minutes)
A volunteer should read the following passage from 2 Chronicles aloud, then group members should read the analysis silently.

[5]Then Jehoshaphat stood up in the assembly of Judah and Jerusalem at the temple of the LORD in the front of the new courtyard [6]and said:

"O LORD, God of our fathers, are you not the God who is in heaven? You rule over all the kingdoms of the nations. Power and might are in your hand, and no one can withstand you. [7]O our God, did you not drive out the inhabitants of this land before your people Israel and give it forever to the descendants of Abraham your friend? [8]They have lived in it and have built in it a sanctuary for your Name, saying, [9]'If calamity comes upon us, whether the sword of judgment, or plague or famine, we will stand in your presence before this temple that bears your Name and will cry out to you in our distress, and you will hear us and save us.'

[10]"But now here are men from Ammon, Moab and Mount Seir, whose territory you would not allow Israel to invade when they came from Egypt; so they turned away from them and did not destroy them. [11]See how they are repaying us by coming to drive us out of the possession you gave us as an inheritance. [12]O our God, will you not judge them? For we have no power to face this vast army that is attacking us. We do not know what to do, but our eyes are upon you."

This powerful prayer of Jehoshaphat, king of Judah, exhibits several elements of good intercession. First, the intercession is made in the context of the king's resolve to inquire of the Lord concerning a serious military threat by the Moabites and Ammonites (verses 2-4). He proclaims a fast and assembles the people from all over Judah. In other words, he prepares for intercession.

His first words to God announce God's identity as *the God who is in heaven*. "O LORD, God of our fathers, are you not the God who is in heaven?" Compare this statement with the opening of the Lord's Prayer: "Our Father in heaven. . . ."

Then Jehoshaphat declares two of God's attributes: His *power and might* and His *rulership* of the kingdoms of the nations. By doing this, Jehoshaphat builds one side of his case on the fact that God is able to defeat the threatening enemy. He even gives an example of how God showed His power in the past. He goes on to use that example to remind God of His promise to save them when they cry to Him for help.

This reminder to God leads Jehoshaphat into the other side of his case. This side is built on another attribute of God: His *justice*. Jehoshaphat announces to God that the very nations God prohibited the Israelites from invading are now trying to drive them out of the "possession you gave us as an inheritance." He appeals to both God's justice and His promise.

Jehoshaphat has established his case. In summary, it is: God, You are able to defeat the enemy (You have the power), and God, You should defeat the enemy (You are just). Thus Jehoshaphat is ready to present his request: "O our God, will you not judge them?"

The closing statement is probably very pleasing to God. First, Jehoshaphat affirms the people's total dependence upon God. They simply do not have the power to face the enemy. Second, he affirms their trust in God. "We do not know what to do [our dependence], but our eyes are upon you [our trust]."

What a great prayer! And it is answered! Immediately, the Spirit of God speaks to them through Jahaziel and says, "Do not be afraid or discouraged because of this vast army. For the battle is not yours, but God's." God then gives them instructions for the battle. Jehoshaphat and the people fall down and worship God and in faith obey God by marching against the enemy. There they find that God has caused the enemy to destroy one another. Not only does God answer the prayer to defeat the enemy, He gives them a wealth of plunder from the enemy.

5. Briefly share your own thoughts on this prayer.

Focusing on God's Character

❖ PART B ❖

ANOTHER PRAYER (15 minutes [9 sessions] or 10 minutes [16 sessions])

Nehemiah was a Jewish official in the Persian court while the Persians controlled much of the Middle East, including Israel. He prayed the following prayer when he received news that the Jewish remnant in Jerusalem was in great trouble and disgrace because the wall of Jerusalem had been broken down.

> [4]When I heard these things, I sat down and wept. For some days I mourned and fasted and prayed before the God of heaven. [5]Then I said:
>
> "O LORD, God of heaven, the great and awesome God, who keeps his covenant of love with those who love him and obey his commands, [6]let your ear be attentive and your eyes open to hear the prayer your servant is praying

before you day and night for your servants, the people of Israel. I confess the sins we Israelites, including myself and my father's house, have committed against you. [7]We have acted very wickedly toward you. We have not obeyed the commands, decrees and laws you gave your servant Moses.

[8]"Remember the instruction you gave your servant Moses, saying, 'If you are unfaithful, I will scatter you among the nations, [9]but if you return to me and obey my commands, then even if your exiled people are at the farthest horizon, I will gather them from there and bring them to the place I have chosen as a dwelling for my Name.'

[10]"They are your servants and your people, whom you redeemed by your great strength and your mighty hand. [11]O LORD, let your ear be attentive to the prayer of this your servant and to the prayer of your servants who delight in revering your name. Give your servant success today by granting him favor in the presence of this man." (Nehemiah 1:4-11)

6. Analyze this prayer and consider the following:

a. What was Nehemiah's request?

b. List the attributes of God that Nehemiah presented in his prayer.

c. Discuss how Nehemiah used these qualities of God to present his case for God to grant his request.

A PRAYER FOR OUR TIME (5 minutes)

A volunteer should read the following aloud.

A British woman, Sandra, was temporarily living in Holland. She needed a job, but she was faced with a major problem: she spoke no Dutch! Who would hire an English-speaking laboratory technician?

One of Sandra's friends, who had been meditating on God as the Creator, prayed:

> O God, You are the Creator of the heavens and the earth. All around me are evidences of Your creativity. You have made everything so perfectly and beautifully. God, You are so good at creating! You must truly enjoy creating things, even now.
>
> And so, Creator God, I ask You to do some creating today. I ask You to create a job for Sandra—a job that is made just for her. I praise You that You can do this, and that it would delight Your heart to do this work of creativity.

This situation actually happened. Soon after this prayer, Sandra got an interview at a place where there were no jobs. After the interview, Sandra reported that the supervisor had spent over an hour talking with her. He then said, "Sandra, I owe you an apology. There are no jobs here. I only took the interview to practice my English. But now, I've decided to make a job here for you."

GROUP PRAYER (25 minutes [9 sessions] or 30 minutes [16 sessions])

7. As a group, select one of the following titles or attributes as the focus of your meditation: God's greatness; Jehovah-Jira (The LORD Provides); God is compassionate; El Shaddai (The All-sufficient One); The LORD is holy.

8. For about ten minutes, silently meditate on the selected title or attribute, focusing on what God is really like. Then ask God, "In light of who You are, what would *You* like to do?"

You may have noticed that you have not been asked to discuss your prayer concerns. This omission was made so that your central focus of prayer might be who God is. From that focus you may then draw in your own concerns.

9. When each member of the group is ready, come together and pray. Keep your prayers brief and focused on what you learned during your meditation time.

FINAL THOUGHT
The depth of our intercession is related to the depth of our understanding of God and His character. As we meditate on God's titles and attributes, we can grasp what He desires to do. Then our prayers are based primarily on who God is, not on what we see as human needs.

Paul's prayer in Colossians 1:9 (PH) is appropriate for us as we venture into intercession that focuses on God's character:

We are asking God that you may see things, as it were, from his point of view by being given spiritual insight and understanding.

ASSIGNMENT
10. Daniel 9:4-19 records a prayer of Daniel concerning the desolation of Jerusalem. Read this prayer, as well as its context, by reading all of Daniel 9.

11. Analyze this prayer.

a. What was Daniel's request?

b. List the attributes of God that Daniel presented in his prayer.

c. How did Daniel use these qualities of God to present his case for God to grant his request?

12. In your intercession this week, first focus on God's titles and attributes. It would be good to explore a variety of these titles and attributes throughout the week, but you may find that you are led to stay with one of these qualities for several days.

13. In light of your thoughts on the character of God, ask Him: "What would You like to do?" concerning the issues you are praying about.

14. Read the "Prayer Focus" section of study 4.

15. Answer this question before the next session: What have you seen God do this week?

STUDY FOUR

FOCUSING ON GOD'S KINGDOM VALUES
Acts 4

❖ PART A ❖

SHARING (15 minutes)

1. What have you seen God do during this past week? Relate one or more items you recorded in exercise 15 of last session's assignment.

2. What happened this past week during your times of prayer when you tried to focus on God's character? Recount some of your experiences.

3. Write down one thing you learned from this discussion.

Remember that only groups in the 16-session track should do the shaded sections of this study.

THE PRAYER FOCUS: *Focusing on God's Kingdom Values*
(15 minutes [9 sessions] or 20 minutes [16 sessions])

As human beings we are influenced by three realms:

a. The natural or physical realm, where we spend seventy to eighty years in a human body. The values of the natural realm are such things as food, clothing, health, and finances.
b. The realm or kingdom of darkness, where the forces of evil are in control. The values of the kingdom of darkness are such things as lying, stealing, killing, cheating, addictions, abuses, and immorality.
c. The Kingdom of God, where God through Christ rules the hearts and lives of people. The values of the Kingdom of God are such things as love, faith, hope, peace, unity, forgiveness, boldness, and holiness.

Jesus' lifestyle, teachings, and prayers all focus on the values of the Kingdom of God. He said, "I have told you these things, so that in me you may have peace. In this world you will have trouble. But take heart! I have overcome the world" (John 16:33). Our Lord was more concerned that His followers live with inner peace (a quality of His Kingdom), than that they have a trouble-free life.

Jesus' followers learned to value what Jesus valued. In Acts 4, Peter and John's lives were threatened. They were warned, "not to speak or teach at all in the name of Jesus." This was a serious threat to their physical well-being. They called a prayer meeting. Their prayer revealed that they valued the advancement of God's Kingdom more than their own physical safety. Not once did they ask for physical protection. Their one request was for boldness, a quality of God's Kingdom.

There are thirty prayers recorded in the New Testament. Only two of these mention physical needs. We should not ignore the needs we and others have in the physical realm, but we need to be careful not to let them be the major thrust of our prayers.

It is also interesting to see how seldom the kingdom of darkness is mentioned in the New Testament prayers. In

Matthew 6:13, Jesus prayed, "And lead us not into temptation, but deliver us from the evil one." Again in His high priestly prayer, recorded in John 17, Jesus prayed for the disciples by asking, "Holy Father, protect them by the power of your name" (John 17:11).

After describing spiritual warfare in Ephesians 6:10-18, Paul tells us to pray. Prayer is not part of the armor. Prayer is the battlefield. Paul does not ask us to pray *against* the powers of darkness. Instead he says, "Keep on praying *for* all the saints."

What are we to pray? In verses 19-20, Paul tells us what he wanted them to pray for himself. "Pray also for me, that whenever I open my mouth, words may be given me so that I will fearlessly make known the mystery of the gospel, for which I am an ambassador in chains. Pray that I may declare it fearlessly, as I should." His request shows that his concern was for the advancement of God's Kingdom.

One of the lessons from the New Testament prayers is that we should focus much more on the values of the Kingdom of God than on physical needs or on the kingdom of darkness. "But seek first his kingdom and his righteousness, and all these things will be given to you as well" (Matthew 6:33).

4. Share one thought that stood out to you from this reading.

THE PRAYER: Acts 4:23-31 (15 minutes)
A volunteer should read this passage from Acts 4 aloud, then group members can read the analysis silently.

> 23On their release, Peter and John went back to their own people and reported all that the chief priests and elders had said to them. 24When they heard this, they raised

their voices together in prayer to God. "Sovereign Lord," they said, "you made the heaven and the earth and the sea, and everything in them. [25]You spoke by the Holy Spirit through the mouth of your servant, our father David:

"'Why do the nations rage
    and the peoples plot in vain?
[26]The kings of the earth take their stand
    and the rulers gather together
against the Lord
    and against his Anointed One.'

[27]Indeed Herod and Pontius Pilate met together with the Gentiles and the people of Israel in this city to conspire against your holy servant Jesus, whom you anointed. [28]They did what your power and will had decided beforehand should happen. [29]Now, Lord, consider their threats and enable your servants to speak your word with great boldness. [30]Stretch out your hand to heal and perform miraculous signs and wonders through the name of your holy servant Jesus."

[31]After they prayed, the place where they were meeting was shaken. And they were all filled with the Holy Spirit and spoke the word of God boldly.

The Christians in Jerusalem offered this prayer to God after the Jewish leaders had commanded Peter and John not to speak or teach in the name of Jesus. This threat was a response to their healing of the crippled beggar and subsequent bold preaching of Jesus' resurrection.

To appreciate the surprising attitude of these Christians, it might be helpful to project yourself into this group. How would you respond to Peter and John's report of their encounter with the Jewish leaders? Considering what these same leaders had done with Jesus, wouldn't you feel deep fear, almost panic? Wouldn't you want to pray earnestly for God's physical protection from this threat? Wouldn't you want to ask God for a new strategy that would be less offensive to these powerful men?

But these Christians asked for none of these things. Instead, they opened their prayer by first proclaiming the sovereignty and creative nature of God. Then they reviewed some history concerning the struggle between God and rebellious man and how God was the one in control. Up to this point we might have prayed similarly.

But, instead of asking God to use that power and control to protect them, their request was, "enable your servants to speak your word with great boldness. Stretch out your hand to heal and perform miraculous signs and wonders through the name of your holy servant Jesus." They were asking God to *continue* to empower them to speak boldly and perform wonders. It's as though they said, "Lord, you've got them on the ropes. Let us follow you as you go in to strike the knockout blow."

They saw this whole series of events from the perspective of the Kingdom of God; not from their own interests of protection. God loves such praying. He answered immediately! "After they prayed, the place where they were meeting was shaken. And they were all filled with the Holy Spirit and spoke the word of God boldly."

Perhaps our prayers would be answered in such a fashion if we were to reach into the mind of God and discover His heart. With the Kingdom of God as our focus, we will be praying Kingdom-expanding prayers.

5. Briefly share your own thoughts on this prayer.

ASSIGNMENT
▶ Work through the "Other Prayers" section in Part B of this study by reading the Scripture and following the instructions.
▶ Answer this question before the next session: What have you seen God do this week?

Focusing on God's Kingdom Values

❖ PART B ❖

OTHER PRAYERS (15 minutes [9 sessions] or 10 minutes [16 sessions])

6. Identify the values of the Kingdom of God prayed for in each of these passages.

Luke 22:31-32

John 17

Ephesians 1:15-23

Ephesians 3:14-21

7. Can you think of any other values of God's Kingdom from Scripture?

A PRAYER FOR OUR TIME (5 minutes)
A volunteer should read the following aloud.

Suppose your church is going through difficult times. Several members are struggling financially. Others are having health problems. Besides praying for these specific needs, what else might you pray? Consider the following prayer for your church:

Sovereign and gracious Lord, nothing is hidden from You. You see the spiritual needs, while I can see only the physical. As much as I desire that my brothers and sisters have good health and finances, I am asking You to use their circumstances to conform them more to the image of Christ.

May their nonChristian friends see the difference You make in the midst of suffering.

You allowed Job to suffer physically in order that he might eventually be able to say, "My ears had heard of you but now my eyes have seen you."

O compassionate Father, use these temporary hardships to bring eternal good into the lives of my friends. May they be strengthened with all power according to Your glorious might so that they may have great endurance and patience, and joyfully give thanks to You, Father. As the result of Your working in their inner being during these difficulties, may all those who observe them give You praise and glory.

See Colossians 1:11-12.

GROUP PRAYER (25 minutes [9 sessions] or 30 minutes [16 sessions])
8. Briefly share current situations where you or other Christians are in difficulty. Spend a couple of minutes in silence, asking God to put on your heart what you should pray.

9. Spend some time in group prayer, lifting these situations to the Lord.

FINAL THOUGHT
The essence of this session's teaching is that when we pray, "Give us each day our daily bread," we need to pray that phrase within the context of the stronger imperative, "Your Kingdom come, Your will be done." Daily bread is essential for physical life, but God's Kingdom and His will are essential for spiritual and eternal life. Our prayers should reflect the centrality of God's Kingdom in this world and our lives.

ASSIGNMENT
10. Find some other Scriptures that might help you pray in the realm of God's Kingdom.

11. In your intercession this week, consider how to pray in the realm of God's Kingdom for the situations you are concerned about. Use Scriptures covered in this lesson and ones you have discovered to give your intercession substance.

12. Write down the requests God leads you to make that relate to the Kingdom of God.

13. Read the "Prayer Focus" section of study 5.

14. Answer this question before the next session: What have you seen God do this week?

FOCUSING ON GOD THROUGH STRATEGIC PRAYING
John 17

❖ PART A ❖

SHARING (15 minutes)

1. What have you seen God do during this past week? Relate one or more items you recorded in exercise 5 of last session's assignment.

2. What happened this past week during your times of prayer when you tried to focus on God's Kingdom values? Recount some of your experiences.

3. Write down one thing you learned from this discussion.

Remember that only groups in the 16-session track should do the shaded sections of this study.

> **GROUP PRAYER (10 minutes)**
> Pray together, focusing on God's Kingdom values.

THE PRAYER FOCUS: *Focusing on God Through Strategic Praying* (15 minutes [9 sessions] or 20 minutes [16 sessions])

We have two advocates. Jesus is our advocate to the Father, like a lawyer pleading our case before Him. Jesus is this kind of high priest because He "has been tempted in every way, just as we are—yet was without sin" (Hebrews 4:15). Therefore, He can sympathize with us. He goes to the Father and says such things as, "Father, when people are tired physically, it affects their emotions, as well as their ability to grasp spiritual things and to see things as they are." He represents our case to the Father.

Our other advocate is the Holy Spirit. He represents the Father's views and thoughts to us. Jesus said in John 16:13 that when the Spirit comes, "He will not speak on his own; he will speak only what he hears." The Holy Spirit represents the Father in order to bring about the Father's desires on earth. He tells us what God is thinking.

Intercession is like these two advocates. Sometimes intercession is taking man's needs and presenting them to the Father. At other times intercession is taking the Father's desires and praying for those things to be done on earth. The Bible is clear about many of God's desires. As intercessors we should learn to pray in such a way that His desires are being fulfilled on earth.

For instance, in 1 Timothy 2:3-4 Paul says, "This is good, and pleases God our Savior, who wants all men to be saved and to come to a knowledge of the truth." There is a parallel passage in 2 Peter 3:9 that says God does not want "anyone to perish, but everyone to come to repentance." Knowing this is God's desire, how do we pray?

If we say, "Father save the world," then we throw the entire responsibility on God. God wants us to co-labor with Him in intercession. We do this by discovering those things that will *cause* God's desire to be accomplished.

John 17 is a good example. The Father desired that the world would believe His Son was sent by Him. Jesus did *not* pray, "Father make the world believe that You sent me." Such a prayer would have thrown all the responsibility on the Father. What He did pray was "that all of them [His followers] may be one, Father, just as you are in me and I am in you.

48

May they also be in us so that the world may believe that you have sent me" (John 17:21). He had discovered and prayed that which would *cause* God's desire to be accomplished.

The most difficult part of intercession is taking the time and effort to discover what to pray. Asking is the easy part. An intercessor needs to know what the Scriptures say about God's desires and then prayerfully seek what will cause those desires to happen on earth.

Another example of Jesus praying a strategic prayer rather than putting all the responsibility on God occurred when Peter was being severely tempted by Satan. Jesus could have prayed, "Father, rescue Peter." Or He could have simply rebuked Satan. Jesus told Peter, "But I have prayed for you, Simon, that your faith may not fail" (Luke 22:32). By praying thus, God's desire for Peter's life had the greatest possibility of being accomplished. The answer to that prayer had an impact not only on Peter, but also on the church.

Praying from God's desires means first of all knowing what God's stated desires are in the Bible, then taking the time to discover the most strategic request to give God toward the fulfillment of His desire.

Most of the time when Paul tells churches what he prays for them, he states what he prays and then what he believes that request will accomplish. For example, in Philippians 1 Paul wants these people to live pure and blameless lives. So what does he pray? "This is my prayer: that your love may abound more and more in knowledge and depth of insight" (Philippians 1:9). But he prays this "so that" among other things they will be pure and blameless. Paul knew God's desire was that Christians be pure and blameless. Leviticus 11:45 says, "be holy, because I am holy." He prayed something that would help cause holiness.

4. Share one thought that stood out to you from this reading.

THE PRAYER: *John 17* (15 minutes)

⁶"I have revealed you to those whom you gave me out of the world. They were yours; you gave them to me and they have obeyed your word. ⁷Now they know that everything you have given me comes from you. ⁸For I gave them the words you gave me and they accepted them. They knew with certainty that I came from you, and they believed that you sent me. ⁹I pray for them. I am not praying for the world, but for those you have given me, for they are yours. ¹⁰All I have is yours, and all you have is mine. And glory has come to me through them. ¹¹I will remain in the world no longer, but they are still in the world, and I am coming to you. Holy Father, protect them by the power of your name—the name you gave me—so that they may be one as we are one. . . .

²⁰"My prayer is not for them alone. I pray also for those who will believe in me through their message, ²¹that all of them may be one, Father, just as you are in me and I am in you. May they also be in us so that the world may believe that you have sent me. ²²I have given them the glory that you gave me, that they may be one as we are one: ²³I in them and you in me. May they be brought to complete unity to let the world know that you sent me and have loved them even as you have loved me.

²⁴"Father, I want those you have given me to be with me where I am, and to see my glory, the glory you have given me because you loved me before the creation of the world.

²⁵"Righteous Father, though the world does not know you, I know you, and they know that you have sent me. ²⁶I have made you known to them, and will continue to make you known in order that the love you have for me may be in them and that I myself may be in them." (John 17:6-11,20-26)

This powerful prayer is rich with implications of God's desires. One of God's desires that appears several times is that people would believe God sent Jesus into the world. In verse 8 Jesus prayed, "They knew with certainty that I came from you, and they believed that you sent me." God's desire that Jesus' disciples believe was fulfilled. In verse 21 Jesus prayed, "that the world may believe that you have sent me" and in verse 23, "to let the world know that you sent me." The same objective recurs, this time in reference to the whole world. For the Son of God to request this repeatedly should lead us to believe that this was (and is) an important desire of God.

Notice that Jesus did not ask the Father directly to fulfill this desire. Instead, He prayed for two things that would cause the world to believe:

▶ Spiritual protection (verse 11)
▶ Unity among the disciples (verses 21 and 23)

In verse 11 He prayed, "Holy Father, protect them by the power of your name." Why? "So that they may be one as we are one." Spiritual protection would produce unity among the disciples.

But what does unity have to do with the world believing? Verses 21 and 23 both make the connection. In verse 21 Jesus prayed "that all of them may be one, Father, just as you are in me and I am in you. May they also be in us so that the world may believe that you have sent me." And in verse 23 He prayed, "May they be brought to complete unity to let the world know that you sent me and have loved them even as you have loved me."

We may summarize the cause and effect chain with this diagram:

Cause 1: "Protect them by your name"

↓

[SO THAT]

↓

Cause 2: "They may be one"

↓

[SO THAT]

↓

God's Desire: "The world may believe"

5. Briefly share your own thoughts on this prayer.

Focusing on God Through Strategic Praying
❖ PART B ❖

OTHER PRAYERS (15 minutes [9 sessions] or 10 minutes [16 sessions])

6. For the following prayers from Scripture, identify God's desire(s) and the cause(s) that fulfill that desire. (Circle "that," "so that," or "in order that" as key words.)

[16]I pray that out of his glorious riches he may strengthen you with power through his Spirit in your inner being, [17]so that Christ may dwell in your hearts through faith. And I pray that you, being rooted and established in love, [18]may have power, together with all the saints, to grasp how wide and long and high and deep is the love of Christ, [19]and to know this love that surpasses knowledge—that you may be filled to the measure of all the fullness of God. (Ephesians 3:16-19)

Causes:

God's Desires:

[9]And this is my prayer: that your love may abound more and more in knowledge and depth of insight, [10]so that you may be able to discern what is best and may be pure and blameless until the day of Christ, [11]filled with the fruit of righteousness that comes through Jesus Christ—to the glory and praise of God. (Philippians 1:9-11)

Causes:

God's Desires:

⁹For this reason, since the day we heard about you, we have not stopped praying for you and asking God to fill you with the knowledge of his will through all spiritual wisdom and understanding. ¹⁰And we pray this in order that you may live a life worthy of the Lord and may please him in every way: bearing fruit in every good work, growing in the knowledge of God, ¹¹ being strengthened with all power according to his glorious might so that you may have great endurance and patience, and joyfully ¹²giving thanks to the Father, who has qualified you to share in the inheritance of the saints in the kingdom of light.
(Colossians 1:9-12)

Causes:

God's Desires:

A PRAYER FOR OUR TIME (5 minutes)
A volunteer should read the following aloud.

Suppose you have been a prayer partner with Linda, a missionary, for several months. You receive a letter from Linda in which she confesses she has been feeling spiritually empty for some time. She says that although her faith remains strong and her mission work is going well, she has been seeing her ministry as an ordinary job consisting of ordinary tasks. Consider the following portion of a prayer for Linda. (See Ephesians 3:18-19.)

> Father, as I consider Your servant Linda, I am reminded of Your desire for all Your children that Paul wrote in his letter to the Ephesians. He prayed that they "may be filled to the measure of all the fullness of God." I believe You want to fill Linda to the measure of all the fullness of God. And Lord, Paul prayed that these Christians at Ephesus might "have power, together with all the saints, to grasp how wide and long and high and deep is the love of Christ, and to know this love that surpasses knowledge." He saw that as they received this power to know and experience Christ's love, they would be filled with Your fullness. So, I want to pray that Linda will receive this same power to comprehend and experience Christ's love. Won't You pour Your Spirit of power and love into her heart in a new and deep way just now? Won't You fulfill Your desire to fill Linda with all of Your fullness? Thank you for hearing this request that is according to Your will.

GROUP PRAYER (25 minutes [9 sessions] or 30 minutes [16 sessions])
7. As a group, list some of God's desires found in the following Scriptures.

Matthew 28:18-20

Luke 18:1

John 6:40

1 Thessalonians 4:3

1 Thessalonians 5:18

1 Peter 2:15

8. Select one of these desires of God that is appropriate for
   you. Spend five minutes in silence, reflecting on the question, "What do you and others in the group need to pray
   to 'cause' God's desire to be fulfilled?"

9. Spend a few minutes praying together and lay these
   requests before God.

FINAL THOUGHT

As intercessors, we need to get our prayer requests from God.
The next time you are asked to pray for an event or for someone's salvation, health, etc., stop and ask, "Lord, what are
Your desires, and what can I pray that will cause Your desires
to take place?"

ASSIGNMENT

10. Identify other Scriptures revealing God's desires.
    Determine what causes might fulfill those desires.

11. In your intercession this week, try to determine God's
    desires that are related to the areas of your intercession.
    Where appropriate, pray for the causes that might fulfill
    those desires.

12. Find some letters from missionaries that you could bring to subsequent sessions. These letters may provide good substance for your group prayer.

13. Read the "Prayer Focus" section of study 6.

14. Answer this question before the next session: What have you seen God do this week?

FOCUSING ON GOD THROUGH WAITING
Psalm 62

❖ PART A ❖

SHARING (15 minutes)

1. What have you seen God do during this past week? Relate one or more items you recorded in exercise 5 of last session's assignment.

2. What happened this past week during your times of prayer when you tried to focus on God through strategic praying? Recount some of your experiences.

3. Write down one thing you learned from this discussion.

Remember that only groups in the 16-session track should do the shaded sections of this study.

GROUP PRAYER (10 minutes)
Pray together, focusing on God through strategic praying.

THE PRAYER FOCUS: *Focusing on God Through Waiting*
(15 minutes [9 sessions] or 20 minutes [16 sessions])

How is one to pray when Scripture does not clearly state God's desires? How do we know what to say to God at times when we or others are in grief, pain, or sorrow?

David can help us. He is best known for his many victories as king of Israel, yet he spent about ten years in a disheartening situation.

Anointed king as a young man, David seemed to have everything going his way. He killed Goliath and soon people were singing: "Saul has slain his thousands, and David his tens of thousands" (1 Samuel 18:7). God had already rejected Saul as king. Now all He had to do was simply remove him. But instead God allowed Saul to remain in office and to be filled with hate toward the anointed king. Because of this situation, David had to live as a fugitive for years.

On the surface, it looked as though God had said one thing to David, but worked in a different direction. It would have been easy for David to become bitter. Instead David wrote some of his greatest psalms during those agonizing years.

In Psalm 62, David revealed one of the secrets of his life—an essential truth for those who would know God's mind amid situations beyond our understanding. He wrote,

> My soul waits in silence for God only;
>   from Him is my salvation. . . .
> My soul, wait in silence for God only,
>   for my hope is from Him. (Psalm 62:1,5; NASB)

There are several ways of waiting on God, but no doubt the most intense is waiting in silence. Waiting in silence is an important aspect of intercession. It gives God an opportunity to give His thoughts to us. Psalm 62 closes with two thoughts that God spoke to David during his silence: "Power belongs to God" and "Lovingkindness is Thine, O Lord." David could not have been assured of this had he not taken time to listen to God.

In Jeremiah 42:1-4 we read that the remnant of Judah came to Jeremiah saying, "Pray that the LORD your God will tell us where we should go and what we should do." And

Jeremiah responded, "I will certainly pray to the LORD your God as you have requested; I will tell you everything the LORD says and will keep nothing back from you." Note that Jeremiah prayed to listen to God. If God is going to be central in our praying, we must learn to listen as well as talk to Him.

When we listen to God, we can be sure what is spoken will never contradict the Scriptures. In fact, most of what God speaks to us will be pure Scripture. He may remind us of a passage or a thought from Scripture, or He may take us to a passage we had never thought of before. Before leaving the earth, Jesus said the Holy Spirit would come and "remind you of everything I have said to you" (John 14:26).

If you have never practiced the discipline of silence before God, you will have to learn to grow in this discipline. Tell God about a situation or need, then ask Him to speak. At first, wait in silence for one minute. As you are able, extend the time of silence to two or three minutes, or even more.

We are not talking about Eastern religion here. Most Eastern meditation puts the mind in neutral and lets any thoughts come. When the Bible talks about silence before God or biblical meditation, it speaks of a focal point that is either God Himself or the Scriptures. In that setting God's voice can best be heard. He makes something clear by an impression or a reminder of a previous thought or Scripture.

During the 1970s, Hans Kristian smuggled Bibles into Russia. Once he was caught and put in jail to await interrogation. He wrestled in prayer because he so desperately did not want to go to prison. In his book, *Secret Invasion*, Hans said, "Now that I quit talking to Him He began speaking to me. The verse flashed into my mind; who for the joy set before him endured the cross."[1] Through this experience, Hans's will became one with God's, and he had great peace. He began reading his Bible, and a passage came alive for him. Of this he says,

> Isaiah had penned that prophesy almost 3,000 years before, but in my heart I knew that in some mysterious way it was God's promise to me at that very moment. The thought was not wishful thinking, a vain hope, a straw that I was grasping at in desperation—but something I

knew. A few moments before I had been in despair, gripped by the fear of languishing in prison, and now I knew with absolute certainty that I would be set free. The living God, the maker of heaven and earth, had communicated this assurance to my heart.[2]

God waited until Hans quit talking before He communicated to Hans. Then, God communicated His thoughts to Hans through the Scriptures.

The best place to listen to God is in a group setting where everyone is listening to God about the same subject or need. After a period of silence, the group can start sharing impressions they received. After one person shares, see if others have had the same or similar impressions. As you do this, you can come to a consensus of what God has communicated to you. There is great safety in such communications.

4. Share one thought that stood out to you from this reading.

THE PRAYER: *Psalm 62* (15 minutes)

[1]My soul waits in silence for God only;
From Him is my salvation.
[2]He only is my rock and my salvation,
My stronghold; I shall not be greatly shaken.
[3]How long will you assail a man,
That you may murder him,all of you,
Like a leaning wall, like a tottering fence?
[4]They have counseled only to thrust him down from his high position;
They delight in falsehood;
They bless with their mouth,
But inwardly they curse.
[5]My soul, wait in silence for God only,
For my hope is from Him.

[6]He only is my rock and my salvation,
My stronghold; I shall not be shaken.
[7]On God my salvation and my glory rest;
The rock of my strength, my refuge is in God.
[8]Trust in Him at all times, O people;
Pour out your heart before Him;
God is a refuge for us.
[9]Men of low degree are only vanity,
And men of rank are a lie;
In the balances they go up;
They are together lighter than breath.
[10]Do not trust in oppression,
And do not vainly hope in robbery;
If riches increase, do not set your heart upon them.
[11]Once God has spoken;
Twice I have heard this:
That power belongs to God;
[12]And lovingkindness is Thine, O Lord,
For Thou dost recompense a man according to his work.
    (Psalm 62, NASB)

The primary focus of this session is to wait in silence before the Lord. Thus, the specific content of this prayer is not the central focus—David's announcement to God of his intention to wait in silence is.

As stated above, David makes this announcement twice in this psalm, in verses 1 and 5. In the first case he follows with "from Him is my salvation," and in the second with "for my hope is from Him." David seems to be saying, "I'm not doing well, but You are my only hope. Therefore, I'm just going to wait for You to lead me out of this mess."

This response resembles that of the disciples to Jesus when many followers were deserting Him. He asked the Twelve if they wished to go away too. Simon Peter said, "Lord, to whom shall we go? You have the words of eternal life" (John 6:68).

David continues to support his reason for waiting by stating who God is to him: God is his rock, his salvation, his fortress, his refuge, his strength. Finally, he affirms that God is both strong and loving, and that He will reward each person according to what he has done (He is just). Then David waits in silence.

5. Briefly share your own thoughts on this psalm.

Focusing on God Through Waiting

❖ PART B ❖

ANOTHER PRAYER (15 minutes [9 sessions] or 10 minutes [16 sessions])

> ¹Out of the depths I cry to you,
>   O Lord;
>   ²O Lord, hear my voice.
> Let your ears be attentive

to my cry for mercy.
³If you, O LORD, kept a record of sins,
O Lord, who could stand?
⁴But with you there is forgiveness;
therefore you are feared.
⁵I wait for the LORD, my soul waits,
and in his word I put my hope.
⁶My soul waits for the Lord
more than watchmen wait for the morning,
more than watchmen wait for the morning.
⁷O Israel, put your hope in the LORD,
for with the LORD is unfailing love
and with him is full redemption.
⁸He himself will redeem Israel
from all their sins. (Psalm 130)

6. a. What is the attitude of the psalmist?

b. How does he affirm the importance of waiting?

A PRAYER FOR OUR TIME (5 minutes)

The steering committee of a large local church is confronted with a request by the outreach committee to establish a church service, separate from the regular ones, that would appeal to the unchurched in the community. This proposal for a different service would require considerable resources (personnel, space, and money).

The steering committee decides to set aside a day for prayer. The prayer includes much praise and thanksgiving, and it affirms God's sovereignty over the future of their church. The prayer then turns to this issue of a new service. Finally, the prayer leader prays, "Lord, we now seek You in silence. We wait for Your word. Give us ears to hear."

The committee members then spend two hours alone and in silence. When they gather again, they share what they have heard. One member says Isaiah 43:18-19 has been a recurring theme: "Forget the former things; do not dwell on the past. See, I am doing a new thing! Now it springs up; do you not perceive it?" Another member says that as she considered the possible loss of resources on the foreign mission program, she was struck with the order of church growth indicated in Acts 1:8, when Jesus told the disciples that they would be "witnesses in Jerusalem, and in all Judea and Samaria, and to the ends of the earth." She feels their church needs to put a priority on their "Jerusalem," the local community.

Finally, a member who has been negative about this new venture confesses he spent the initial portion of his silence thinking of Scriptures that would oppose this action. He says he thought of Scriptures like Ephesians 4:14, which instructs us not to be "tossed back and forth by the waves, and blown here and there by every wind of teaching" that is in vogue at the time. But he began to see he was not being silent. As he quieted himself, Luke 5:37-38 came strongly to mind: "And no one pours new wine into old wineskins. If he does, the new wine will burst the skins, the wine will run out and the wineskins will be ruined. No, new wine must be poured into new wineskins."

Any one of these insights could be attributed to human thinking, or even manipulation, but together they presented a strong, unified case. The steering committee decided to recommend that the church begin the new service.

7. How did God use the silence of these elders?

8. Briefly discuss some issues you are facing that seem neutral with regard to God's Word. (An example could be the issue of whether or not to change employment.)

9. Select one of these issues on which the group may focus.

10. Enter a short time of prayer, followed by several minutes of silent waiting.

11. As a group, share any insights you received during the time of silence. Do not force the issue by creating "messages" just to show unity. The amount of time given to this exercise may be too brief for members to hear from God. The assignment below may provide a continuation of this experience.

FINAL THOUGHT

As you wait in silence, be patient with yourself. The discipline of silence is a difficult one—one that requires an active mind focused on God and His Word, yet a mind that is submissive to listening rather than insistent on telling.

ASSIGNMENT

12. Lamentations 3:26 uses the Hebrew word translated "waits in silence" in Psalm 62. Read Lamentations 3:19-28.

13. Analyze this passage. Look for the elements it has in common with Psalm 62, such as a statement of the writer's situation, a declaration of one or more qualities of God, and an affirmation of waiting silently.

14. In your intercession this week, work on the discipline of waiting silently before the Lord, beginning with short segments of silence and trying to expand these segments as the week progresses.

15. Record any messages you think you are receiving from the Lord. (If your group wishes, you may choose a common issue that the entire group agrees to focus on throughout the week. Perhaps it will be a continuation of the focus of your group prayer during this session. When you compare notes next week, you may discover that you have all received a similar message from the Lord.)

16. Read the "Prayer Focus" section of study 7.

Notes
1. Hans Kristian and Dave Hunt, *Secret Invasion*, formerly titled *Mission: Possible* (Eugene, OR: Harvest House Publishers, 1975), pages 48-49.
2. Kristian and Hunt, pages 48-49.

FOCUSING ON GOD WITH PERSEVERANCE
Isaiah 64

❖ PART A ❖

SHARING (15 minutes)
1. What happened this past week during your times of prayer when you tried to focus on God through waiting? Did you receive any impressions?

2. Write down one thing you learned from this discussion.

GROUP PRAYER (10 minutes)
Pray together, focusing on God's response to your waiting in silence.

THE PRAYER FOCUS: *Focusing on God with Perseverance*
(15 minutes [9 sessions] or 20 minutes [16 sessions])
One of the great biblical prayers is recorded in Isaiah 63–64. In it, Isaiah pleads with God to graciously look upon His people

once again. The focus of this session is found in the final phrase of Isaiah 64:4. The verse reads:

> Since ancient times no one has heard,
>> no ear has perceived,
> no eye has seen any God besides you,
>> who acts on behalf of those who wait for him.

The Hebrew word translated *wait* means to adhere to or to cling to. Perhaps one of the best pictures of this kind of waiting is in Genesis 32, where Jacob wrestles with the angel of the Lord and says, "I will not let you go unless you bless me." Isaiah affirms that God responds to that kind of an attitude.

Throughout history, the saints who have seen the greatest works of God have had to wait on God. Abraham was promised a son through whom God would bless all nations. It took twenty-five years before that son was born. Jacob was blessed by his father Isaac. Twenty years passed before he began to see God's blessing on his life. Joseph had a dream from God but it was years later, after enslavement and imprisonment, that the dream came true. Hannah went to the temple "year after year" pleading for a child. Ten years passed after David was anointed as king before he was crowned.

Probably each person using this workbook has been praying about something for years and yet has seen little happen up to now. Habakkuk had such an experience. He cried out to God,

> How long, O LORD, must I call for help,
>> but you do not listen?
>> (Habakkuk 1:2)

Later God answered:

> For the revelation awaits an appointed time;
>> it speaks of the end
>> and will not prove false.
> Though it linger, wait for it;
>> it will certainly come and will not delay.
>> (Habakkuk 2:3)

George Mueller said that once he knew something was God's will he never quit praying for it until God gave it. We are told that he prayed daily for two of his nonChristian friends for over fifty years before they were saved. It is always too soon to quit. Our God acts on behalf of those who wait for Him, who cling to Him, who will not let go of Him.

One of the greatest acts of faith is not to give up on God. During those years of waiting God often seems very inactive. But we are assured in Isaiah 30:18,

> Yet the LORD longs to be gracious to you;
>> he rises to show you compassion.
> For the LORD is a God of justice.
>> Blessed are all who wait for him!

Jesus "told his disciples a parable to show them that they should always pray and not give up" (Luke 18:1). That parable was about a widow who kept going back to a judge until he gave her her request.

To maintain God-focused or God-centered praying, we need to develop the discipline of clinging to God when nothing seems to be happening. Let God know you will not let go of Him.

3. Share one thought that stood out to you from this reading.

THE PRAYER: *Isaiah 64* (15 minutes)

> [1]Oh, that you would rend the heavens and come down,
>> that the mountains would tremble before you!
> [2]As when fire sets twigs ablaze
>> and causes water to boil,
> come down to make your name known to your enemies
>> and cause the nations to quake before you!

71

³For when you did awesome things
    that we did not expect,
    you came down,
    and the mountains trembled before you.
⁴Since ancient times no one has heard,
    no ear has perceived,
no eye has seen any God besides you,
    who acts on behalf of those who wait for him.
⁵You come to the help of those who gladly do right,
    who remember your ways.
But when we continued to sin against them,
    you were angry.
    How then can we be saved?
⁶All of us have become like one who is unclean,
    and all our righteous acts are like filthy rags;
we all shrivel up like a leaf,
    and like the wind our sins sweep us away.
⁷No one calls on your name
    or strives to lay hold of you;
for you have hidden your face from us
    and made us waste away because of our sins.
⁸Yet, O LORD, you are our Father.
    We are the clay, you are the potter;
    we are all the work of your hand.
⁹Do not be angry beyond measure, O LORD;
    do not remember our sins forever.
Oh, look upon us, we pray,
    for we are all your people. (Isaiah 64:1-9)

Isaiah's prayer actually begins somewhere in chapter 63, either in verse 7 or in verse 14. In this first part of the prayer, Isaiah tells of the cycle of history that is so much a part of Israel: (1) God has performed goodness out of His compassion and kindness; (2) the people have rebelled and grieved His Holy Spirit; (3) God has sent His judgment upon Israel.

Then Isaiah implores the Lord to redeem Israel by appealing to the fact that He is their Father and that "our Redeemer from of old is your name" (Isaiah 63:16). He calls for a mighty appearance of the Almighty: "Oh, that you would rend the heavens and come down" (64:1).

Isaiah follows this call with a description of the living, Holy God that distinguishes Him from every other god. One of His distinguishing features is that He "acts on behalf of those who wait for him" (64:4). As stated above, this waiting involves a clinging to God, a holding on until God responds. Isaiah is inviting his readers to wait for God with him.

In the remainder of the prayer, Isaiah declares that the people are unworthy of God's salvation because "all our righteous acts are like filthy rags" (64:6). However, he returns to his appeal for God's redemption on the simple basis that "we are all your people" (64:9). On that basis, Isaiah perseveres.

4. Briefly share your own thoughts on this prayer.

ASSIGNMENT

▶ Read the Scripture in the "Another Prayer" section in Part B of this study.
▶ Answer this question before the next session: What have you seen God do this week?

Focusing on God with Perseverance
❖ PART B ❖

REVIEW (15 minutes)

▶ Share what you have seen God do this past week. Relate one or more items you recorded in exercise 2 of last session's assignment.
▶ Review together the primary ideas of this study's "Prayer Focus" section.

ANOTHER PRAYER (15 minutes [9 sessions] or 10 minutes [16 sessions])

[1]Sing joyfully to the LORD, you righteous;
    it is fitting for the upright to praise him.
[2]Praise the LORD with the harp;
    make music to him on the ten-stringed lyre.
[3]Sing to him a new song;
    play skillfully, and shout for joy.
[4]For the word of the LORD is right and true;
    he is faithful in all he does.
[5]The LORD loves righteousness and justice;
    the earth is full of his unfailing love.
[6]By the word of the LORD were the heavens made,
    their starry host by the breath of his mouth.
[7]He gathers the waters of the sea into jars;
    he puts the deep into storehouses.
[8]Let all the earth fear the LORD;
    let all the people of the world revere him.
[9]For he spoke, and it came to be;
    he commanded, and it stood firm.
[10]The LORD foils the plans of the nations;
    he thwarts the purposes of the peoples.
[11]But the plans of the LORD stand firm forever,
    the purposes of his heart through all generations.
[12]Blessed is the nation whose God is the LORD,
    the people he chose for his inheritance.
[13]From heaven the LORD looks down
    and sees all mankind;
[14]from his dwelling place he watches
    all who live on earth—
[15]he who forms the hearts of all,
    who considers everything they do.
[16]No king is saved by the size of his army;
    no warrior escapes by his great strength.
[17]A horse is a vain hope for deliverance;
    despite all its great strength it cannot save.
[18]But the eyes of the LORD are on those who fear him,
    on those whose hope is in his unfailing love,
[19]to deliver them from death

74

and keep them alive in famine.
^{20}We wait in hope for the LORD;
    he is our help and our shield.
^{21}In him our hearts rejoice,
    for we trust in his holy name.
^{22}May your unfailing love rest upon us, O LORD,
    even as we put our hope in you. (Psalm 33)

The final three verses of this psalm contain the same Hebrew word for wait that is used in Isaiah 64. The psalmist is convinced that the proper action for God's people to take is to "wait in hope," to cling to God.

5. How might Psalm 33:1-19 lead the psalmist to affirm that waiting in hope is the right thing to do?

A PRAYER FOR OUR TIME (5 minutes)
Suppose that your friend Janet married Tom when they were both nonChristians. A couple of years later, Janet received Christ and immediately began praying for Tom to do the same. However, four years have passed, and Tom still shows no sign of coming to Christ. He is not hostile to Christianity (although he shows some irritation when aggressively confronted by Christians), but he is simply not interested in spiritual matters.
    Consider the following prayer that you might pray for Janet and Tom:

Lord God, a God who deeply cares for every person, for You have created them all in love, I lift up Tom to You as one of those whom You love deeply. You say in Your Word that You desire that all people be saved and come to the knowledge of the truth; therefore You desire that Tom be saved and come to the knowledge of the truth. This is Your will, so I confidently plead for his salvation.
    Lord Jesus, as You taught Your disciples to keep on praying with perseverance and to keep on asking with

persistence, I declare that I will cling to You and Your promises until You bless me by answering my request. As the widow continually kept coming to the judge with her request, I will follow Your teaching to keep coming to You on Tom's behalf. Thank You that You will also plead Tom's case with the Father.

GROUP PRAYER (25 minutes [9 sessions] or 30 minutes [16 sessions])
6. Discuss some difficult situations in your lives in which God seems to be silent.

7. As a group, decide on one or two of these situations to pray together about.

8. Pray together, spending at least ten minutes on the situation(s).

FINAL THOUGHT
Focusing on God's desires with perseverance obviously requires much patience. We cannot insist on an answer in our own timing. We may be called to cling to God persistently for years. But remember these two things:

▶ God sometimes requires us to wait with perseverance (Habakkuk 2:3, Zephaniah 3:8).
▶ God blesses those who persevere in waiting for Him (Isaiah 64:4, Daniel 12:12).

How we pray depends primarily on what we believe about God: Is He faithful? Is He just? Does He act on behalf of those who wait for Him? If we believe these qualities about God, we will persistently come back to Him no matter how long it takes.

You who call on the LORD,
    give yourselves no rest,
and give him no rest. (Isaiah 62:6-7)

ASSIGNMENT
9. In 1 Samuel 1, we read of a woman named Hannah who persevered with the Lord concerning her desire to bear a

son. Her prayer is recorded in verse 11, but her ongoing attitude of persistence is seen throughout the whole chapter. Read this chapter, and note Hannah's disposition toward the Lord.

10. Consider the difficult situations in your life or the life of one for whom you are praying. Make a list of those situations about which God seems to be silent. For each item on the list, pray to the Lord by telling Him that you are going to wait in hope, to cling to Him regarding that need.

11. As you are led, practice persisting in prayer for the situations you have listed.

12. Continue to pray for the situations the group prayed for during the session.

13. Read the "Prayer Focus" section of study 8.

14. Answer this question before the next session: What have you seen God do this week?

STUDY EIGHT

FOCUSING ON GOD BY PRAYING HIS WORD
1 Kings 8

❖ PART A ❖

SHARING (15 minutes)
1. What have you seen God do during this past week? Relate one or more items you recorded in exercise 6 of last session's assignment.

2. What happened this past week during your times of prayer when you tried to focus on God with perseverance?

3. Write down one thing you learned from this discussion.

GROUP PRAYER (10 minutes)
Pray together, focusing on God with perseverance.

THE PRAYER FOCUS: *Focusing on God by Praying His Word* (15 minutes [9 sessions] or 20 minutes [16 sessions])
One of the greatest statements in the Bible is 1 John 5:14-15—

This is the confidence we have in approaching God: that if we ask anything according to his will, he hears us. And if we know that he hears us—whatever we ask—we know that we have what we asked of him.

There is a simple progression in this statement. First, we ask according to God's will. This causes God to hear us. And when God hears us, He answers whatever we have asked.

In this passage, the key to receiving what we ask is to ask according to God's will. We desire many things but are uncertain whether they are God's will. But one thing is always certain: the words God speaks. Whatever He has declared in Scripture is His will. When we pray Scriptures back to God, we can be certain we will receive what we are asking.

Charles Finney lived in the early 1800s. He was an attorney who became an evangelist. He came to know Christ primarily by reading Scripture. He had absolute confidence in the Word of God. Sometimes he would pray, "I hope that thou dost not think that I can be denied. I come with thy faithful promises I cannot be denied." When we rest our case upon the very words of God, our request cannot and will not be denied.

We see this in the great prayers of intercession in the Bible. In Exodus 32, Moses intercedes for Israel after they had made their golden calf. He says in verse 13, "Remember your servants Abraham, Isaac and Israel, to whom you swore by your own self: 'I will make your descendants as numerous as the stars in the sky and I will give your descendants all this land I promised them, and it will be their inheritance forever.'" After Moses quoted God's own words, the very next verse says, "Then the LORD relented and did not bring on his people the disaster he had threatened."

When Nehemiah heard of the desolate situation in Jerusalem, he prayed intensively for about four months. His prayer is summarized in Nehemiah 1:5-11. At the heart of his prayer he says,

"Remember the instruction you gave your servant Moses, saying, 'If you are unfaithful, I will scatter you among the nations, but if you return to me and obey my commands, then even if your exiled people are at the farthest horizon, I will gather them from there and bring them to the place I have chosen as a dwelling for my Name.'" (Nehemiah 1:8-9)

Throughout the book of Nehemiah he prays eleven times. He never mentions the wall in his prayers. Nehemiah's main concern is not a wall around Jerusalem but that the people will be brought back together. That is why he reminds God of what He said to Moses. Was Nehemiah's prayer answered? Yes, a large number of Israelites came back and were united in Jerusalem. The fulfillment started with a man bringing God's Word in prayer to God.

Daniel's great prayer of intercession is quoted in Daniel 9. Why did he pray as he did? Daniel tells us why in verse 2: "In the first year of his reign, I, Daniel, understood from the Scriptures, according to the word of the LORD given to Jeremiah the prophet, that the desolation of Jerusalem would last seventy years." Daniel knew his prayer would have to be answered because he was responding to the very words of God. His prayer was one of great humility. We do not threaten God with His Word, but we humbly ask Him to carry out that which He Himself has spoken.

There are two basic ways to pray Scripture. The first is to allow God to initiate the conversation. The most straightforward way to do this is to have a Bible-reading program where each day you ask God to speak to you through His Word. As you are prayerfully reading, mark those things that stand out to you. Then go back and talk to God about those thoughts He has spoken. In such a conversation with God, you might ask Him questions or make statements of agreement with Him. In this process, you may be led to confess something or to ask Him to do something for you or someone else. Or, you may be led to offer praise to God from your heart of thanksgiving. The better you know the Scriptures, the deeper the conversation will go. Often when you interact with God over His Word, other scriptures will flood your mind as the Spirit of God brings them to your remembrance. Then you can respond to those scriptures as well and go deeper in your conversation.

A second way to pray over Scripture is for you to initiate God's words. As you are talking with God about a certain request, bring Scripture into your conversation. It might be one of the prayers in the Bible or a statement in the Bible. Take care that you do not simply search for scriptures that support your desire without considering whether those scriptures apply to your situation. This kind of "proof-texting" is like putting words in God's mouth.

One of the best ways to keep God central in your intercession is to use His own thoughts, His words, to convey your request.

4. Share one thought that stood out to you from this reading.

THE PRAYER: 1 *Kings 8* (15 minutes)

²²Then Solomon stood before the altar of the LORD in front of the whole assembly of Israel, spread out his hands toward heaven ²³and said:

"O LORD, God of Israel, there is no God like you in heaven above or on earth below—you who keep your covenant of love with your servants who continue wholeheartedly in your way. ²⁴You have kept your promise to your servant David my father; with your mouth you have promised and with your hand you have fulfilled it—as it is today. ²⁵Now LORD, God of Israel, keep for your servant David my father the promises you made to him when you said, 'You shall never fail to have a man to sit before me on the throne of Israel, if only your sons are careful in all they do to walk before me as you have done.' ²⁶And now, O God of Israel, let your word that you promised your servant David my father come true. . . .

³³"When your people Israel have been defeated by an

enemy because they have sinned against you, and when they turn back to you and confess your name, praying and making supplication to you in this temple, [34]then hear from heaven and forgive the sin of your people Israel and bring them back to the land you gave to their fathers. . . ."

[54]When Solomon had finished all these prayers and supplications to the LORD, he rose from before the altar of the LORD, where he had been kneeling with his hands spread out toward heaven. [55]He stood and blessed the whole assembly of Israel in a loud voice, saying: [56]"Praise be to the LORD, who has given rest to his people Israel just as he promised. Not one word has failed of all the good promises he gave through his servant Moses." (1 Kings 8:22-26,33-34,54-56)

The setting of King Solomon's prayer is the dedication of the Temple in Jerusalem. Before he prays in front of the people, he sets the focus by a speech in which he begins, "Praise be to the LORD, the God of Israel, who with his own hand has fulfilled what he promised with his own mouth to my father David" (1 Kings 8:15). He follows that statement with the actual words God spoke.

The prayer follows this speech and contains the same focus: God's words and promises. In verse 24 he says, "You have kept your promise"; "with your mouth you have promised and with your hand you have fulfilled it." In verse 25 he asks God to "keep . . . the promises" He made to David. In verse 26, he repeats that request.

The remainder of the prayer repeatedly alludes to God's covenant. Verses 33 and 34 imply that God responds positively to the people's confession, turning back to God, and supplication to Him—that He will listen to them, forgive them, and restore them to their land. Throughout this prayer, Solomon appeals to God's covenant with Israel.

Solomon follows his prayer with more praise to God before the assembly. Again he refers to God's word and promises. In verse 56 he says, "Not one word has failed of all the good promises he gave through his servant Moses."

Solomon knew how to pray the Scriptures.

5. Briefly share your own thoughts on this prayer.

Focusing on God by Praying His Word
❖ PART B ❖

ANOTHER PRAYER (15 minutes [9 sessions] or 10 minutes [16 sessions])

In Nehemiah 9, the Levites confess the sins of Israel. They offer this prayer after many days of hearing Ezra read the Book of the Law of God (some or all of the first five books of the Bible).

⁵And the Levites . . . said: "Stand up and praise the LORD your God, who is from everlasting to everlasting."

"Blessed be your glorious name, and may it be exalted above all blessing and praise. ⁶You alone are the LORD. You made the heavens, even the highest heavens, and all their starry host, the earth and all that is on it, the seas and all that is in them. You give life to everything, and the multitudes of heaven worship you. ⁷You are the LORD God, who chose Abram and brought him out of Ur of the Chaldeans and named him Abraham. ⁸You found his heart faithful to you, and you made a covenant with him to give to his descendants the land of the Canaanites, Hittites, Amorites, Perizzites, Jebusites, and Girgashites. You have kept your promise because you are righteous. . . .

¹³"You came down on Mount Sinai; you spoke to them from heaven. You gave them regulations and laws that are just and right, and decrees and commands that are good. ¹⁴You made known to them your holy Sabbath and gave them commands, decrees and laws through your servant Moses. ¹⁵In their hunger you gave them bread from heaven and in their thirst you brought them water from the rock; you told them to go in and take possession of the land you had sworn with uplifted hand to give them. ¹⁶But they, our forefathers, became arrogant and stiff-necked, and did not obey your commands. ¹⁷They refused to listen and failed to remember the miracles you performed among them. They became stiff-necked and in their rebellion appointed a leader in order to return to their slavery. But you are a forgiving God, gracious and compassionate, slow to anger and abounding in love. Therefore you did not desert them. . . .

²⁹"You warned them to return to your law, but they became arrogant and disobeyed your commands. They sinned against your ordinances, by which a man will live if he obeys them. Stubbornly they turned their backs on you, became stiff-necked and refused to listen. ³⁰For many years you were patient with them. By your Spirit you

admonished them through your prophets. Yet they paid no attention, so you handed them over to the neighboring peoples. [31]But in your great mercy you did not put an end to them or abandon them, for you are a gracious and merciful God. [32]Now therefore, O our God, the great, mighty and awesome God, who keeps his covenant of love, do not let all this hardship seem trifling in your eyes—the hardship that has come upon us, upon our kings and leaders, upon our priests and prophets, upon our fathers and all your people, from the days of the kings of Assyria until today. [33]In all that has happened to us, you have been just; you have acted faithfully, while we did wrong. (Nehemiah 9:5-8,13-17,29-33)

6. a. What *direct* references to God's Word and His promises are made?

b. What *indirect* references to His Word and promises are made?

A PRAYER FOR OUR TIME (5 minutes)

Suppose your Christian supervisor at work has been an oppressive manager. Consider the following prayer in which you talk with God concerning this situation:

Lord, I come to You with my concern for Jane, my supervisor. When You walked on this earth as a man, You set the example of being a servant to others (Mark 10:45), even though You had every right to demand the service of anyone You encountered. Your teachings were filled with a call to serve one another. In Luke 22:26, You said: "The greatest among you should be like the youngest, and the one who rules like the one who serves." I believe that for Jane's sake, You want her to develop the heart of a servant as she leads in this area of Your work.

You inspired Paul to write about how masters should handle slaves, that they should treat them with respect and with fairness. I am reminded of how Paul appealed to Philemon in his treatment of Philemon's slave, Onesimus. It thus seems right that a Christian supervisor should treat a Christian employee with that love and consideration to which Paul called Philemon to treat Onesimus.

Please work in Jane's heart and give her Your counsel concerning Your will for her as a Christian leader. May You receive glory and praise as others see how Christians can work together in love and harmony.

Until You choose to change Jane, please help me to have the attitude of Christ, who took the form of a servant and humbled Himself even unto death on the cross (Philippians 2). May I see that I am really working for You and therefore want to work with all my heart (Colossians 3:23-24).

GROUP PRAYER (25 minutes [9 sessions] or 30 minutes [16 sessions])
  7. Briefly discuss concerns that you would like the group to pray for together.

  8. For ten to fifteen minutes, pray for these concerns. As you are prompted, bring Scripture into your prayers and try to discern what God might be saying to the group about the concerns for which you are praying.

FINAL THOUGHT
The words of Christ Himself give us the essence of this session's teaching: "If you remain in me and my words remain in you, ask whatever you wish, and it will be given you" (John

15:7). As the words of Christ our Lord enter our hearts and influence our thoughts and our lives, then our words to Him will enter His heart and influence His actions.

ASSIGNMENT

9. Read through any passage of Scripture you desire. Hopefully, you are already in a program of Bible reading that you may use for this assignment.

   a. Specifically ask God to speak to you through His Word.

   b. Mark those statements in the passage that stand out to you. Then ask God what He might be saying to you personally in these statements. Record any responses you think may be from God.

10. Consider any requests you have been praying to God (as well as those the group has been praying), and bring Scripture into the conversation. Record any results of this conversation.

11. Briefly review the first eight studies of this workbook. For each session write a statement giving the central truth that God revealed to you.

▶ Study 1: Introduction to God-Focused Intercession

▶ Study 2: Focusing on God Through Praise

▶ Study 3: Focusing on God's Character

▶ Study 4: Focusing on God's Kingdom Values

▶ Study 5: Focusing on God Through Strategic Praying

▶ Study 6: Focusing on God Through Waiting

▶ Study 7: Focusing on God with Perseverance

12. Answer this question before the next session: What have you seen God do this week?

CONTINUING IN GOD-FOCUSED PRAYER

During this session we will review what we have covered in the first eight studies. Then we want to give God the opportunity to clarify your next step in your venture in prayer.

SHARING (20 minutes)

1. What happened this past week during your times of prayer when you tried to focus on God by praying His Word?

2. Spend about ten minutes sharing some of the central truths that you recorded in exercise 5 of last session's assignment.

CONVICTIONS (15 minutes)

3. Spend about fifteen minutes individually recording:

a. One to three convictions you now have concerning prayer that you didn't have before you started this study.

b. Bible passages that best summarize these convictions for you.

c. Commitments that God would have you make.

GROUP PRAYER (30 minutes)
  4. Let a member of the group share one of the commitments he or she recorded. Then pray for that member, asking God to fulfill his or her commitment. Go around the group until you have prayed for each person.

5. If you have extra time, go around the group a second time to pray for another of each person's commitments.

FUTURE PLANS (10 minutes)

Discuss how you might help one another in your commitments to prayer. Consider continuing as a group or in smaller subgroups (perhaps in pairs). Consider other possibilities of how you might be accountable to one another in prayer.

FINAL THOUGHT

We hope the conclusion of this workbook is only the beginning of a deepened walk of prayer for you. We trust that you are now committed to a more God-focused lifestyle of prayer. May God Himself, through His Spirit, continue to train you in the ministry of prayer.

SMALL-GROUP MATERIALS FROM NAVPRESS

BIBLE STUDY SERIES

CRISISPOINTS FOR WOMEN
DESIGN FOR DISCIPLESHIP
GOD IN YOU
GOD'S DESIGN FOR THE FAMILY
INSTITUTE OF BIBLICAL
   COUNSELING SERIES

LIFECHANGE
LIFESTYLE SMALL GROUP SERIES
LOVE ONE ANOTHER
STUDIES IN CHRISTIAN LIVING
THINKING THROUGH DISCIPLESHIP

TOPICAL BIBLE STUDIES

Becoming a Woman of
   Excellence
Becoming a Woman of Freedom
The Blessing Study Guide
Celebrating Life
Growing in Christ
Growing Strong in God's Family
Homemaking
Intimacy with God

Loving Your Husband
Loving Your Wife
A Mother's Legacy
Surviving Life in the Fast Lane
To Run and Not Grow Tired
To Walk and Not Grow Weary
What God Does When Men Pray
When the Squeeze Is On

BIBLE STUDIES WITH COMPANION BOOKS

Bold Love
From Bondage to Bonding
Hiding from Love
Inside Out
The Masculine Journey
The Practice of Godliness
The Pursuit of Holiness

Secret Longings of the
   Heart
Transforming Grace
Trusting God
What Makes a Man?
The Wounded Heart
Your Work Matters to God

RESOURCES

Curriculum Resource Guide
How to Lead Small Groups
Jesus Cares for Women
The Small Group Leaders
   Training Course

Topical Memory System (KJV/NIV
   and NASB/NKJV)
Topical Memory System: Life
   Issues (KJV/NIV and
   NASB/NKJV)

VIDEO PACKAGES

Abortion
Bold Love
Hope Has Its Reasons
Inside Out

Living Proof
Parenting Adolescents
Unlocking Your Sixth Suitcase
Your Home, A Lighthouse